Young in America: New Orleans

A Collection of Writings From the Students of Urban League College Track

Perfectly Scientific Press
www.perfscipress.com

Copyright © 2012 by Perfectly Scientific Press

All Rights Reserved. No part of this book may be reproduced, used, scanned, or distributed in any printed or electronic form or in any manner without written permission except for brief quotations embodied in critical articles and reviews.

Cover design by Emily Buford.

Book formatting and processing by Max Jacobs and Debi Dewar.

ISBN: 978-1-935638-27-8

www.psipress.com

Printed in the United States of America

9 8 7 6 5 4 3 2 1

Foreword

At Urban League College Track (ULCT) we believe that brilliance, passion, and creativity are not determined by zip code; educational outcomes shouldn't be either. *Young In America: New Orleans* is a snapshot of the genius that resides within each College Track scholar. The contributing writers are all participants in ULCT, an after-school program that empowers students from underserved communities to reach their dream of earning a college degree. Our mission is to close the achievement gap and create college-going cultures for students who are historically and currently underrepresented in higher education.

Urban League College Track is one of six College Track programs nationwide and the first center outside of California. Our site, ULCT, is a collaborative partnership between the Urban League of Greater New Orleans and College Track. What began four years ago with 39 high school freshmen has grown to serve more than 150 students, grades nine through twelve. This May marks an important milestone in our program's history: We will graduate our first class of college-bound high school seniors.

One of the most important skills our students will take with them to college is the ability to write. No one can refute the fact that writing is an essential part of academic and professional success. The English teacher in me has always sought to give students the basic tools needed to write well. In the first year of my teaching career, that's what I *attempted* to do. I taught grammar and punctuation rules. We diagrammed sentences and discussed parts of speech. Luckily for me and for my students, I left teaching after one year and went to graduate school.

College changed the way I taught. There, I was introduced to strategies such as writing workshops and portfolio assessments. Like a sharp puppy that had mastered a few new tricks, I was eager to get back into the classroom and "show off" to resistant spectators. "I hate writing," was the mantra most of my students had meditated on for much of their school lives. And they had every reason to hate writing. Writing is hard work. It requires focus and revision: Intently seeing the world in which we live and our place within it anew. Writing is cathartic and revolutionary. Unfortunately, the way in which it is often taught in school stifles many students and teachers because by design, most classrooms are neither cathartic nor revolutionary. But that does not mean that they can't be. In my former classrooms I extended the invitation for my students to "write for your life." For nearly two decades students from New Orleans to New York City to Oakland eagerly accepted the invitation.

In school, students "write for a grade." Urban League College Track is not a school and students do not receive grades; they write for a greater purpose. Their writing is powerful, evocative, and bold; it provides a transparent look into what it means to come of age in pre- and post-Katrina New Orleans. Whether a student is in a classroom receiving a grade or in an afterschool program where grades are not assigned, what is critical is that students are able to attach greater meaning to their writing. Just as my former students learned to "write for your life," ULCT students write to voice their thoughts, to concretize their hopes, to subjugate their struggles, and to assert their values.

After 17 years of teaching, I still know a few tricks. I still believe very strongly in writing workshops and portfolios. I maintain that writing is an important academic skill. I have also come to understand that writing is much more than an academic exercise; it is a tangible expression of our being. It is my hope that as you read *Young in America: New Orleans*, you experience who our students *are*.

Sherdren Burnside

Site Director

Urban League College Track,

New Orleans

Introduction

There's no way around the fact that teaching students to write is hard. It takes a long time and there's no quick way to respond. You can't score an essay with a Scantron or true-false answer keys. However, our lack of investment catches up, and it's the students, especially those from underserved communities, who ultimately pay. As a former college teacher, I've witnessed the shock and frustration of freshmen who, after receiving top marks in local high schools, entered first year essay classes without the skills to keep up. So far behind, many of these students withdrew. College was simply too late and too demanding for catching up on basic skills. We often hear the catchphrase *writing as process*; however, I'm not convinced that we regularly model our own advice. Sadly, the reality of high school teacher workloads usually prohibit multiple drafts and one-on-one mentoring—precisely what writing students most need.

So I am grateful to Richard Crandall for his generous offer to fund a book of student writing and to editor Max Jacobs for shepherding us through this process. Thanks also to our colleagues, Dr. Evelyn Hamilton and Rachel Patton, for their help in preparing the manuscript. *Young in America: New Orleans* has offered us this chance to practice what we preach. This book has been a process. It has motivated students to write about their world, their experiences and vision—subjects that matter to them. The project has given both my director Sherdren and me the opportunity to deeply consider our students' work and to push them to produce their best.

In preparing their writing for publication, Urban League College Track (ULCT) students have responded to feedback and produced multiple drafts, editing in the evenings after a full day at school or from home on their own time. They have written not because they had to, but because they wanted to and because someone was offering them an audience for their ideas. Our contributors have evidenced discipline and patience. I am hard-pressed to think of any qualities more important in a writer. I am very proud of them.

The writing here is not merely a recycling of the students' schoolwork. Each piece has been achieved above and beyond our students' regular academic load. While some of the work here was written independently by students, most of the pieces in this volume were produced either in ULCT's Creative Writing class or specifically for this volume. Some of the work originally appeared on our literary website, *The Whispering Conscience*. In addition, two seniors revisited their personal statements drafted in ULCT's college advisory courses to better hone their messages about education.

The pieces in this book represent voices and experiences not often heard. There are few national opportunities for high school students to publish, and most public high schools can't afford literary journals. The work here is deeply personal. Even when tied to political and legal subjects, the students are unafraid to reveal themselves. They also reveal the beautiful, resilient, and sometimes disturbing complexity of New Orleans. Such honesty and effort deserves our attention.

Allison Alsup
Writing Instructor
Editor of *The Whispering Conscience*,
Urban League College Track,
New Orleans

The authors

Sophomore **George Aidoo** attends St. Augustine High School where he is on the honor roll. A longstanding member of ULCT's Creative Writing Workshop, George has published on *The Whispering Conscience* website. A prolific writer and an unconventional thinker, George has filled several black spiral notebooks with long stories and numerous poems. Last summer he attended a Creative Writing Workshop for local high school students on the Loyola of New Orleans campus.

Carl Allridge is a sophomore at Warren Easton High School and a former member of the ULCT Creative Writing class. His fable first appeared on *The Whispering Conscience*.

Lanesa Barabino is a sophomore at Warren Easton High School. One of her poems was selected as a winner in the "My Black is Beautiful" contest and her work has been featured on ULCT's *The Whispering Conscience* literary website. Lanesa uses poetry to explore important issues such as death, war, nature and beauty.

Irene Beauvais is an honor roll student and will be graduating from Lake Area New Tech Early College High School and will be attending college in the fall. She has been writing poetry since the seventh grade. She writes to express her feelings and process her emotions. A former member of the ULCT Creative Writing Class, some of Irene's poems have appeared on *The Whispering Conscience* literary website. In addition she will be publishing some of her work through a book project at her school. Last summer, Irene was awarded a scholarship to attend the Young Writer's Workshop at Aspen Summer Words in Aspen, Colorado.

Senior **Briana Brown** is graduating from Eleanor McMain High School and will be attending a Louisiana university this fall. She wrote her first poem at age four. More recently, she has participated in a summer writing workshop at the New Orleans Center for the Creative Arts. She is also a published writer. Briana is passionate about writing as a way to both inspire and entertain, but also writes for her own personal release and self-examination. In college, she plans to study psychology; someday she hopes to write a children's book.

Freshman **Yasmien Brown** attends Lake Area New Tech Early College High School. Yasmien writes to both soothe her mind and to entertain others. She is inspired by the work of Maya Angelou.

Robert Burnside, Jr. is a freshman at the International High School of New Orleans. He frequently writes about being young in America and the problems facing teenagers such as friendship and being true to one's self. He uses his writing as a chance to voice his opinions and to tell adults what's going on with today's youth. He also sees his writing as a chance to reach other students and to encourage them to make better decisions about their lives. Robert enjoys playing basketball, cross-country racing and writing rap lyrics with his friends.

Candace Gautreaux is a Senior at McDonogh 35 Senior High School and will be attending Dillard University in the fall. She wrote her first story in the UNO Charter School Neighborhood Story Project when she was in the 7th grade. She is also the recipient of an Idea Grant from America's Promise Alliance, funds which she has used to start a mentoring program aimed at lowering high school drop out rates and encouraging elementary age girls to stay in school.

Andrew J. Gould is graduating from Lake Area New Tech Early College High School and will be attending a university this fall. He writes poems in order to express his emotions. He also writes hip hop lyrics and draws inspirations from listening to songs about overcoming struggles. He hopes to study music, among other subjects, in college.

Tia Harris is a sophomore at Lake Area New Tech Early College High School where she participates in the volleyball and basketball programs. She enjoys writing poetry.

Kaila Holloway is a sophomore at Benjamin Franklin High School. She has been writing since middle school and receives inspiration from personal experiences and life lessons. Throughout middle school, she was honored to have two poems entitled, "The Skin I'm In" and "Diamond Miner" published in a creative writing book. Kaila also enjoys cooking, baking and dancing.

Janai McGill is currently a sophomore at Lake Area New Tech Early College High School. She has been composing poetry in her spare time for several years and finds that writing helps her to relieve stress. She is a former member of ULCT's Creative Writing class and her work has appeared on website *The Whispering Conscience.*

Herbert Perryman is a junior at the International High School of New Orleans. Through ULCT, he was awarded a scholarship to attend the CIES conference in Montreal and has been a presenter on two educational conference panels. He has also served as a youth planning leader at the Dryades YMCA Christian Values Conference.

Troy Simon is a senior at Sci Academy high school. In the last three years, he has dedicated much of his time to writing a series of personal essays that he hopes will galvanize and vitalize other young readers. He has been a longstanding member of the Creative Writing course at Urban League College Track and several of his works have appeared on ULCT's literary website, The Whispering Conscience. Twice he has been awarded a scholarship to attend the Aspen Summer Words Young Writer's Workshop. He has been awarded a four year scholarship to attend to attend Bard College through the Posse Foundation, one of only ten local students selected from an initial pool of hundreds of nominees.

Honor roll student **Darielle Trotter** is a senior a G.W. Carver High School and will attend a university in the fall. She has participated in advanced level coursework through Bard College's Early College program. She enjoys reading and writing. She is also a member of the Journey Church where she sings and dances during services.

Contents

I	**Essays, Fiction, and Prose**	3

How to Write About New Orleans   5
   Briana Brown

Brown v. Board of Education   9
   Kaila Holloway

My Miracle: From Mentee to Mentor   19
   Candace Gautreaux

Game   27
   Troy Simon

Promised Endeavors   45
   Darielle Trotter

Empowering Our Youth   49
   Herbert Perryman

The Monkey and The Moon   59
  Carl Allridge

The Burden of Life   61
  Nicoi Pierce

Snatch and Run   65
  Troy Simon

II Poetry   83

Initial Thought   85
  Tia Harris

When I Grow Up   87
  George Aidoo

Tangents   89
  George Aidoo

Truth or Hope?   91
  Lanesa Barabino

Cliché 93
Lanesa Barabino

Letter to My Unborn Baby 97
Briana Brown

Lost 99
Andrew Gould

Imperfectly Great Leader 101
Robert Burnside, Jr.

Your Heart Will Be Hard To Grasp 103
Janai McGill

Full of Flight 105
Irene Beauvais

Destruct of Creativity 107
Irene Beauvais

She Watches Me 109
Irene Beauvais

Hurricane 111

Yasmien Brown

Should I Remain 113

Yasmien Brown

Part I

Essays, Fiction, and Prose

How to Write About New Orleans

by Briana Brown

"How to Write About New Orleans" was inspired by Kenyan journalist Binyavanga Wainaina's "How to Write About Africa," a critical postcolonial text she read in school. Briana, like Wainaina, is native to a place often visited but little understood, so her aim was to recreate Wainaina's "rubric or set of instructions" directed at travel writers, but from the perspective of her own city, New Orleans. Like Wainaina, Briana's piece seeks to use irony to break through cliché and myth and expose the real New Orleans. Briana notes that just as with the original, her essay contains a "...sarcastic twist. If followed, the directions will lead the reader to create a typical New Orleans-based piece of writing from the point of view of an 'outsider' of New Orleans." Briana was inspired to write because although she loves her city, "...people often see the only good of New Orleans in

books but not necessarily the whole truth of it. There's more to this city than what is mentioned in textbooks and the media."

* * * * * * *

If you want to write about New Orleans, be sure to include all the flavorful food and festivals and of course, Mardi Gras. The Krewes of Endymion, Bacchus, Rex and Zulu are all great parades to enjoy at carnival time. But does your reader really want to know their history? Do they care to know that the Krewe of Rex parade was originally segregated and meant for socially elite whites only? Do they really care to know that this segregation was why the all-black Krewe of Zulu was created? You may not want to inform your reader that racial play is still at work even now. When talking about the carnival attire, it's alright to talk about the Indian headdresses and feathered boas, but don't go into too much detail for your reader. Refrain from focusing on the attire the rich white male krewe captains wear as they trot along on their horses and toss out doubloons to the screaming crowds. The white silk blouses and white masks may remind some readers of a very different group's clothing.

Instead write about parties and our famous Southern hospitality, safe topics for any season.

It's a must that you incorporate jazz as it is one of the most important aspects of New Orleans. After all, jazz began right here in New Orleans's own Congo Square. Don't leave out Voodoo either because your reader will want to know all the juicy details on that as well. You can write about the beautifully crafted buildings in the French Quarter, but by all means do not focus on the black man's hands who built them. Also avoid the crime that goes on in the city and the statistics of how many people are shot dead every year, as such facts may unnecessarily disturb the reader. And don't focus on the fact that there is more space here holding prisoners in jail than space holding students in college. The hands that once crafted the bars on balconies now grip the steel bars of a prison cell. Such facts will only discourage visitors.

However, feel free to inform your reader about the importance of the Mercedes Superdome that draws tourists from miles around to enjoy concerts and Saints football games! *Who Dat!* But pay no mind to the sign within the shadow of the Superdome that reads "Future Site of the New Orleans Police

Dept. Forensics Lab," for it is not a part of the revitalization of the city, and this sign is nearly completely covered in weeds as it has sat in an empty lot for five years. Please don't reveal to your reader that the city doesn't even have the means to perform fingerprinting analysis for the people they do throw into the jails. Instead, maybe focus on the charming folk art and the museums, as these are located in safe neighborhoods and will help you get to your fairytale ending...

<u>Sample Entry for New Orleans:</u> The streets in the Quarters are filled with beautiful buildings and the fresh scent of beignets and chicory coffee. The people are friendly. The gumbo is great. The music is jazzy. The parades are wildly fun and the football games are exciting. *Laissez les bon temps rouler!*

If you want to write about New Orleans, this is all your reader needs to know.

Brown v. Board of Education

by Kaila Holloway

As I looked around my new classroom at Haynes Academy, I felt like an outcast. I was the only black child in a pool of white. I was ecstatic that I had received a spot in one of the highest ranked schools in Louisiana, but, of course, there was a catch. I would be one of only seven African-American students in my grade. This new school was so different from my normal atmosphere. Until then, my classrooms were almost exclusively black. Everyone had the same skin color, same hair texture, same background, same EVERYTHING.

Now that was all changing. I was attending a predominately white school, where I would be the oddball because of my skin. When I found out that there would only be seven black children in my grade, I automatically assumed that we would all stick together, and all the white kids would stick together. I was pleasantly surprised when I was asked to join in with the Caucasian kids at lunch. Befriending people outside of my race seemed so outlandish before I attended Haynes. But it was so easy to do so at my new school, and I found myself with many new friends. Though I was thankful for every opportunity that came my way, I could not help but wonder, "What if?"

What if I was forced to attend a segregated school, if everyone around me looked the same, and I was not allowed to interact with people of another race or different skin color? What if I did not have a choice of schools to attend, if *I had* to attend my predominately black neighborhood school? Would I ever stop to think why I wasn't allowed to associate with "different" people or attend their schools? Why their schools were bigger and prettier than mine? Why they had newer textbooks and up-to-date equipment? Why they scored so much higher than my classmates and me on standardized tests? When would I realize that I wasn't receiving the same education as the other race? If the NAACP had not taken the *Brown v. Board of Education* case to the United States Supreme Court, these would not just be random thoughts in my head. It would be my reality.

Less than a century ago, African-American children and Caucasian children weren't allowed to attend the same schools. Blacks were considered an inferior race. In order to maintain white privilege, African-American people were deprived of an equal education. The Supreme Court decision that eradicated school segregation and its second-class schools was *Brown v. Board of Education*. This landmark Supreme Court case not only greatly transformed the African-American community, but also the United States as a whole.

This Supreme Court ruling not only desegregated schools throughout the South, but also helped to overturn the "separate but equal" doctrine altogether. The *Brown v. Board of Education* case is considered one of the most significant Supreme Court decisions ever made in America. It served as a catalyst for African-Americans and inspired them to fight for equal rights, paving the way for black people and bettering our community as a whole. After reading through the history, arguments, aftermath and significance of this case, I realized that the *Brown v. Board of Education* decision is more than a piece of history. It has helped to transform me into the person that I am today by giving me opportunities that my ancestors never thought possible.

Brown v. Board of Education was, in fact, five separate cases, but because they raised similar issues, the Supreme Court decided to hear them together as one. The five cases included: *Briggs v. Elliot, Brown v. Board of Education, Gebhart et al. v. Belton et al., Davis et al. v. County School Board of Prince Edwards County, Virginia,* and *Bolling v. Sharp.* In all five cases the NAACP presented evidence from social scientists proving that segregation reduced the self-esteem of black children, and that prejudice emotionally poisoned the children. The cases also challenged the Constitutionality of segregation altogether.

In the state level courts, panels of judges ruled in favor of the existing segregation laws. After losing all five cases, the NAACP decided to take *Brown v. Board of Education* to the Supreme Court of the United States and appointed Thurgood Marshall as their lawyer.

On December 9, 1952, the Supreme Court was to hear the arguments of all five cases, though each would be argued separately. The defendants contended that segregation of schools was in the best interest of the children, and that as long as the facilities were equal, such separation broke no law. Marshall argued that segregation caused irreparable psychological and sociological damage to black students by characterizing them as inferior. He also argued that segregated schools were not equal and could not be made equal, which in turn meant that black students were being deprived of their Fourteenth Amendment rights. When arguments stopped, the judges unanimously decided that the cases were to be reheard ten months later in October 1953.

After the cases were reargued, Chief Justice Warren delivered the majority opinion. In his ruling, Warren asked, "We come then to the question presented: does segregation of children in public schools solely on the basis of race, even though the physical facilities and other 'tangible' factors may be equal, deprive the children of the minority group of equal educational opportunities? We believe that it does.""[1]

"Segregation of white and colored children in public schools has a detrimental effect upon the colored children. The impact

---

[1] Harman, Gary, Roy M. Mersky, and Cindy L. Tate. *Landmark Surpreme Court Cases: The Most Influential Decisions of the Supreme Court of the United States*. New York: Checkmark Books, 2006.

is greater when it has the sanction of the law; for the policy of segregating the races is usually interpreted as denoting the inferiority of the negro group. A sense of inferiority affects the motivation of a child to learn... Whatever may have been the extent of psychological knowledge at the time of *Plessy v. Ferguson*, this finding is amply supported by modern authority. Any language [347 U.S. 483, 495] in *Plessy v. Ferguson* contrary to this finding is rejected. We conclude that in the field of education the doctrine of 'separate but equal' has no place. Separate educational facilities are inherently unequal. Therefore, we hold that the plaintiffs and others similarly situated for whom the actions have been brought are, by reason of the segregation complained of, deprived of the equal protection of the laws guaranteed by the Fourteenth Amendment."[2]

The Separate but equal doctrine was overturned. The Supreme Court decided in favor of the NAACP and granted African-Americans the rights that were guaranteed to them by the Fourteenth Amendment. This Amendment stated that all people born in the United States are citizens of the United

---

[2]Harman, Gary, Roy M. Mersky, and Cindy L. Tate. *Landmark Surpreme Court Cases: The Most Influential Decisions of the Supreme Court of the United States*. New York: Checkmark Books, 2006.

States, and that no state has the right to create laws depriving any citizen of their rights.

Now that the decision was made, each side had to deliver ways that desegregation could be achieved. Marshall suggested that there should be a fixed date by which segregation must end. The defendants suggested that there should not be a timetable and if they desegregated too quickly, Southern whites would withdraw their children and the public school system would collapse. However, the Chief Justice decided that every district should start implementing the integration plans "with all deliberate speed."

It has now been 58 years since Thurgood Marshall argued that segregation was unconstitutional. In truth, desegregation in the South would be stonewalled, and there are still many public schools in New Orleans that appear segregated. But even so, Brown has paved the way for change. Without the *Brown v. Board of Education* case, I would not be able to attend the high school that I attend now, a predominately white school. I would be stuck in my neighborhood school, with no chance of attending the school of my choice. I would be stripped of the rights given to me by the Fourteenth Amendment. I would be looked down upon by whites, who once believed that they were superior to African-Americans. I would not even consider myself equal to whites, according to scientific studies. Without Brown, I wouldn't have the opportunities that I am presented with today such as college, graduate school, and a career based on my intellectual potential. The brave men and women who decided to fight for their rights in this case and the first black children who integrated all-white schools will always be respected and remembered by me.

This case has impacted every life in America, not just those of African-Americans but of every race. It showed that race should not be an important factor in this country, and that people should not be judged solely on their skin color. The *Brown v. Board of Education* case continues to encourage African-Americans to fight for their rights no matter how big or small the issue. It has personally inspired me to dream bring, and not let anybody hold me back. It has taught me that I should not let the color of my skin stop me from achieving my goals. Because of this case, I know that I am receiving the same education as any other race.

The hardships that my ancestors faced have allowed me to have a better life. The people who fought for integration weren't doing it for themselves. They fought so that future generations could have a better future and the rights that they were deprived of as children. Because of the brave men who decided to fight for their constitutional rights, I am able to attend an ethnically diverse school. I consider myself equal to people of other races, and the *Brown v. Board of Education* case taught me that I AM equal to them. I am proud of my heritage and the hardships that my ancestors faced because it shows that with every struggle African-Americans come back stronger than ever. This decision has allowed so many blacks, including me, to succeed in life. I strive for success and work my hardest because I know that my ancestors were held back. I want to make something of myself to show the people who fought for desegregation that their effort has not gone to waste. I learned that I shouldn't be ashamed of who I am and my heritage because of my skin color. This case encourages me to fight for what I believe in. Knowing that my ancestors weren't given the same opportunities as me, makes me want to live for them and do everything that they weren't allowed to do.

My Miracle: From Mentee to Mentor

by Candace Gautreaux

"Here is a boy with five small barley loaves and two small fish, but how far will they go among so many?" proclaimed Andrew, Jesus' disciple.[3] Andrew thought that five loaves and two fish would not be enough to feed the thousands of hungry people who followed Jesus. Hearing that his sacrificial offering was not enough must have made this young boy feel the way I felt many times in elementary and middle school.

In school, I was alienated and ostracized by my peers. I had been retained twice, once in second grade due to major surgery to correct a limb length shortage. Although my absences were excused, my mother felt that I had missed too many days and

---

[3]John 6:9 (New International Version)

needed to be retained. In fourth grade, I did not pass my Louisiana Educational Assessment Program (LEAP) test. I felt like I was the dumb, sickly child in my family. Students, including my younger siblings, would tease me and tell me that I would never make it out of high school. I hated school. I had let my little sister catch up to me. We even shared some of the same classes. Still I was averaging Ds. I needed help from my sister, but was too ashamed to ask. I thought to myself, I'm the big sister. She should be coming to me for help. Slowly, I was giving up on myself.

Sitting in my eighth grade math class in New Orleans, I felt like I had been dropped in the middle of Tokyo. My teacher was speaking, but his words sounded like a foreign language I didn't comprehend.

"Does anyone have any questions?" he asked.

I had a million questions racing in my head, yet not the courage to ask a single one. I would just sit and look around, believing that I was the only one who didn't understand. I was caught between frustration and shame. Raising my hand would mean letting others know how little I understood. Instead of choosing to do something, I opted for the easy way out. I concluded school just wasn't for me. I was done. As soon as I could, I would drop out.

Many students encouraged me to get a General Education Development (GED) credential rather than try to persevere. People would say things like: "If I were in your shoes, I'd drop out" and "You must be the dumb one in the family to let your little sister catch up with you." I wasn't catching on in school. I had insecurities about it and their comments put the icing on the cake. However, when Mr. Fruga, my eighth grade teacher, heard that I wanted to leave school, he pulled me aside. He had been like a father to me—giving me attention, warning me about boys, and motivating me.

Mr. Fruga looked at me with his brown eyes. He ran his hand along his trimmed beard. "I know school seems hard, but you can make it. I believe in you." Mr. Fruga made me promise to do some research on high school dropouts and their chance of success. Little has changed for this group since 2008. In Louisiana, 53 percent of students who enter ninth grade will leave high school without a diploma. Annually their earning potential will be less than $20,000 in an already depressed economy. Having someone to believe in me when I didn't believe in myself saved me from becoming a part of this statistic.

The disciple Andrew was right! Five loaves and two fish were not enough to feed the multitude. Feeding the 5,000 required a miracle and that's exactly what Jesus did for the multitude and for me. My academic skills and willingness to succeed weren't enough to keep me from giving up on school. Having a caring adult who believed in me made all the difference—that was my miracle. I got the courage and strength to believe in myself when I blocked all of the negative comments out and started focusing on my education and myself. Once I did that, I started seeing good results in my academics.

When my principal, Mrs. Mitchell, and Mr. Fruga saw that I was improving, they encouraged me to apply to Urban League College Track, an after-school program for college-bound high school students. For the past four years, I have attended after-school tutoring sessions Monday through Friday even though the program required only three days per week. The extra help I got at ULCT has indeed kept me on track.

While participating in the program, I also seized other opportunities to better my writing skills: I wrote a proposal and received the "My Idea Grant" from America's Promise Alliance to start my mentoring program called the "Mini Butterflies." I started this program for 10 to 13 year old girls to help lower the high school drop out rates. I knew that it was important to reach out to younger girls because eighth grade was a hard time for me. It was when I first began to think of dropping out of school. My academic abilities seemed inadequate because I learned differently and at a different pace. The challenges and setbacks I experienced in school discouraged me.

I didn't believe I was smart enough to go to college. However, at ULCT, I found staff like Mrs. Burnside and Dr. Hamilton who also believed in me and continued to push me to reach my goal of going to college, just like Mrs. Mitchell and Mr. Fruga did in elementary school. My mentors inspired me to pass my miracle forward to my "Mini Butterflies."

The difficulties I faced in school have made me stronger. Even now, I have to work extremely hard to succeed in school. I still attend the Urban League College Track five days a week. I also take a dual enrollment course at Delgado Community

College. My hard work is paying off. In the fall, I will be attending Dillard University. You may be reading this essay and feeling like you can't make it. It's important to shut out the Andrews in your life who say negative things to bring you down. It's important to surround yourself with people who believe in you, push you to do your best, and who lead you on the right path.

> When they had all had enough to eat, Jesus said to his disciples, "Gather the pieces that are left over. Let nothing be wasted." So they gathered them and filled twelve baskets with the pieces of the five barley loaves left over by those who had eaten. After the people saw the sign Jesus performed, they began to say, "Surely this is the Prophet who is to come into the world."[4]

Jesus fed the multitude and still had enough left over to fill twelve baskets. My miracle could have stopped just with me getting the encouragement I needed to stay in school. But it

---
[4] John 6:12-14 (New International Version)

will not! I'll continue to tell others my story and let them know that they too can make it.

Game

by Troy Simon

Raheem had it made. Fine girls and easy money. My cousin had the life that came with freedom, the life that I expected to live someday. He was 16, four years older than me, and didn't bother with school. Raheem was free and knew how to work the system. His momma was living in Baton Rouge, Louisiana. Every once in a while she sent a check. Otherwise Raheem stayed with my grandmother. Sometimes he listened to her and sometimes he didn't.

Gold teeth. Dreadlocks. Tattoos. I liked Raheem's style. He was five foot six with dark skin and light brown eyes. His workouts left his shoulders buff. He wore sagging blue jeans with a white T-shirt and Nikes like the gangsters on TV. Raheem was cool, no worries. I never saw Raheem mad about anything. *I'm not tripping man*, he used to tell me.

More than anything, Raheem ran game and played girls. He told them how beautiful they were. He tricked them into thinking he really meant what he said. These girls were thick and fine with body. They partied fast. He always bragged to me about how he had it *going on*. He had things in *place*. Raheem planned his day by going to the mall, hanging out there, and meeting girls, or sometimes he would chill with his chicks one at a time. It depended on Raheem's mood. He would scroll through his phone and tell me stories about how they were *feeling him*. These girls' minds were gone for my cousin.

"Moon, this one, her name Ciara," he told me. "She was joked out when I told her she was the finest thing in the mall. Her name Rickshell. That thing something serious boy."

He would just go on and on. Raheem hooked up with them for pleasure and a place to lay his head, maybe even a little dinner. I considered Raheem a certified gangsta because he did things in a real way. He showed a dog mentality with no respect or remorse for what he did. Raheem played the game cutthroat. His favorite lines from Lil Wayne went like this:

I will show you the game, teach you the game
and see what you get and peep what you do,
but you will never do it better than me.
You know what I'm talking about.

I liked that slang. Lil Wayne wasn't playing; he was the master. It was the same way I felt about Raheem. I wanted Raheem to show me his game so someday I'd do it better. Then I'd be the gangsta living the life. Or so I thought.

At 12, I figured it was time for me to start getting connected, so I asked Raheem to show me how to run game. I always thought about being a gangsta since I failed at everything else—family and school. I believed my life was better off without school. My momma and I were on bad terms, so I moved in with my grandmother and hoped that things would get better. They didn't. I just brought all my problems with me. My father tried giving me solutions over the phone, but after Katrina, he evacuated to Dallas. Since he split from my momma a couple of years before, we had drifted apart. He wanted to help me, but he had not been around enough to understand my problems. Raheem was who was around.

"Let me hang with you, son," I told my cousin. We were downstairs in the parking lot of the Houston apartment my grandmother was staying in since Katrina. "I mean show me the game, man."

Raheem laughed and called me fake. "Boy, Wanda going to beat you. You know your momma don't play that." He sat back in his chair and cracked his neck. "All right, you come run with me right quick by this l'il chick house."

I jumped in the car. It was a school night, and I didn't tell my grandmother that I was leaving with Raheem. I had no idea who we were going to visit, but I was excited. I wanted to see Raheem in action. I wasn't thinking about homework or studying; what did they matter? I was behind in my academics as usual. I couldn't keep up. I wasn't ever going to make it anyway. I couldn't even read, but Momma wasn't complaining. She was busy running the streets with her friend, Red-Face Dee. She cashed the child support our father sent and bought jewelry, clothes, and shoes. She was doing her own thing; she wasn't checking up on me.

While we were driving, Raheem asked me questions about my experiences with girls. "Boy you don't be on them things at school?" he asked. "I'll have them sprung out over me."

"No, I don't be thinking about them like that." I smiled shyly.

He laughed. "Son, I'm going to put you on game."

When we got to his girlfriend's house, he told me sit down and peep. He told me to watch how she be *digging* him. Teresa was nice—brown skinned with cat eyes and big lips. Gold teeth. Tattoos. Five foot six, she was 15 and still in the eight grade. He told me they knew each other before Hurricane Katrina and were just getting a chance to meet again. He said she was his *little yeah*. When we arrived, I sat in her living room and watched Raheem's every move, listened to Raheem's every word. He talked stupid to her and grabbed her arms behind her back 'til she told him to stop. It was play fighting, but she was loving it.

"See Moon, this how you treat them when they be tripping," he said.

When we got back to my grandmother's house, she was waiting at the door. It was one o'clock in the morning. She was worried about where I went and why I didn't tell her I was leaving.

"I was about to tell you Grandma, but I was too lazy to come up the stairs," I said.

"Don't leave without telling me you left with Raheem, or I will send you back by your momma."

"I told you I didn't mean to do it! You act like you don't understand!"

"Boy, who you yelling at? I would knock you upside your head with this broom!" She screamed and reached for the handle.

I closed my eyes and ducked, placing my hands over my head. "Alright, Grandma. I'm sorry."

I didn't mean to get out of place with her, but I was angry. She kept yelling in my ear. Raheem just laughed at me and shook his head.

At school I thought about what I did the night before. I knew I was changing. I also knew that my grandmother wouldn't like it, but I felt like my own man, someone who had control over his own decisions. I hadn't ever felt that way before.

In the halls, I acted like Raheem. I said what he would say. If a girl walked by, I grabbed her hand. If a girl was talking to her friends, I'd interrupt her and say, *What up sweetie*? If I caught a girl looking my way, I'd ask, *Wuzzam*?

I liked the new me. Girls were laughing and telling me how cute I looked with my dreadlocks and how they had been *wanting to talk* with me. I got my first number that day from a girl name Naomi. I was chatting her up in the hallway and asked her if she had a boyfriend. She told me no. She was red with a few freckles in her face, long dark brown hair and everything I looked for in a girl: Nice shape, attitude, and style. I got other numbers that day too, but there was something special about Naomi.

When I got home, I told Raheem how many numbers I got. He didn't say anything. He refused to speak like he was angry I'd run a better game that day. A few minutes later, he asked me to come with him by some girl named Keedy's house. He had met her in the store. I stopped doing my homework and went with him. He never told me about her, but he said she had a little cousin named Lia he wanted me to hook up with.

When we got there, Lia answered the door and told us Keedy was punished and couldn't see anyone.

Driving away, Raheem cracked his neck and told me, "Moon, never think that these girls are always honest."

So we went over by Teresa's house to hang out for a while. Teresa's friend, Nia, was there. She was short with long hair and light brown eyes. She was mixed: Black, Mexican, and white. Nia said that Teresa had told her all about me, that I was single and cute.

We all sat down in the living room talking while Raheem and Teresa wrestled. They stopped every once in a while to make out. We all talked about Hurricane Katrina and our days. Suddenly, Raheem wandered off down the hall. Teresa followed; she laughed and jumped on his back. I saw that Raheem was making his move, so I knew it was time to make mine. I leaned over on the couch, but unlike Raheem, I was nervous.

"So, what's up?" I asked Nia.

"Nothing."

"What's your name again?" I was trying to play it cool. I remembered her name.

She smiled and repeated her name. "Nia."

"Tell me a little bit about yourself." I twisted my dread locks, just in case she had failed to see them.

She laughed. "I'm 13 and love to get to know people. I'm from Houston and like to sleep." She stared into my eyes. "Now tell me a little bit about you."

"Ain't too much to know really. I'm 12." I swung my dreads slow like I was thinking about something deep and leaned in closer. "I got a lot on my mind."

"Aw, what's on your mind? We can talk about it."

We never even kissed, but sat talking for hours about our family problems and our differences until Raheem was ready to leave. Nia and I exchanged numbers to finish the conversation over the phone. She was a nice girl and didn't mean any harm. She just thought I was the same too.

When Raheem and I left, we stopped back by Keedy's house, but her momma told us she went out with her friends. Raheem shrugged his girl's lie off. Suddenly I realized Raheem wasn't the only one running game.

In school, my rep was high. I'd gone from being the dumb kid who couldn't read to the hottest boy walking the halls.

Naomi didn't like that, so we kept our relationship on the down low. I was talking to her friends, trying to hook up with them, too. Some of them allowed it, and some of them didn't. Naomi knew what was going on, but I told her that I went out with her friends so they wouldn't suspect we were going out together.

"Don't trip, girl," I told her. "You my baby forever." It was a Raheem line. She fell for it.

Before I knew it, I was the master running the game. I was on top. I loved the way my life was going. Golds. Dreads. Girls. I had it made. No one couldn't tell me nothing. I was so good at putting things *in place* that I decided to set my mind on bigger, better boss man things: Money and drugs. That's when I got connected with Raheem's friend. Nick flipped weed. He was 15, red and lanky with a bush. But Nick didn't wear the saggy pants and wife-beaters. His jeans were pulled up, his shirts had sleeves. He was respectful and positive.

We got high every day we were together. I smoked because it made me feel like a man. We only had two customers every few days. Still, I had a little money in my pockets. I was somebody. Nick would look me in the eyes and say, *Keep the faith man. Stay strong.* I'd stare back and we'd fall on the floor laughing.

Once I didn't go home for three days. I'd been hanging at Teresa's house smoking. When I got back to my grandmother's apartment, it was midnight. My grandmother saw a changed person: Blackened lips, red eyes and stale clothes. I was so high that my body hurt. I sat in the corner of my grandmother's living room and fell asleep on the floor.

Late in the afternoon, I woke up with a bad headache. I looked for Raheem, but he was gone. My grandmother told me he went to the mall. She grabbed my hand and demanded that I talk with her privately in her room where my little brother and sisters couldn't hear.

"Moon, what's wrong? Why you haven't been going to school? At first, you was excited about school when you started, but it looks like you got side tracked by Raheem. Tell me, what's the matter?"

I smiled nervously. "Nothing's wrong. I just been hanging with my cousin and Nick. I want to be like this. Raheem didn't ask me; I asked to follow him."

"But why Moon? You was going to school, trying to do right. Now you have been missing days from school, not speaking to your momma and sleeping out. Remember when you told me before the storm how you wanted to change your life? You cried in my arms on North Derbigny Street and I prayed for you and told you that things were going to get better. You had your mind set on change then."

I remembered. Two years before Katrina, I wanted to restart my life. I was in the third grade, fighting a lot at school, getting suspended and skipping class. I was cussing my teachers, throwing desks at them and picking fights with other kids. I wandered the corridors, wrote on the walls and spit on the floors. I was angry. I felt like no one at home cared enough to make sure I was doing well in school. I didn't even understand the point of doing well, and no one tried to convince me otherwise. Both of my parents had dropped out, so what did school matter? It didn't feel like I had someone around to tell me what mattered. My dad wasn't around to discipline me. My mother was trying her best to raise me right, but I was out of control. I didn't listen to anyone.

The school called my mother in for meetings.

"Why doesn't Troy want to go to class? What can we do?" Same questions all the time and always the same answers.

"I can't read."

"Why can't Troy read?"

"I don't know," my mother told them, not wanting to admit that she struggled with reading herself. "He's not paying attention in class."

"Can you help Troy at home?"

"I'll try."

When the meeting was over, they would tell me to go back to class. I would sit in my desk, wait a few minutes and leave. Same routine every day.

That year I often thought about living with my grandmother forever or living on the streets. Sometimes I thought about changing my life, helping my brothers and sisters learn how to read. I believed that everyone was depending on me to show them the way to a better life. I asked my grandmother how I could change. She told me she couldn't change me, but God could. She offered to pray with me every day. She said that prayer *is key*. I would act up in school and go home to pray for deliverance from God before I went to bed. I cried out to God. I thought better about myself. I sat there for hours in my grandmother's arms, letting my problems go. I told her that I was ready to go to school and learn. I told her that I was sorry for all the trouble I caused, for the anger I held in my heart.

"That's alright, things are going to get better," she told me. "Just walk with God."

I took heed to what she said, but ended up back in trouble a few weeks later. The teacher was passing out report cards in class. When she handed me mine, another student jacked my grades. I cussed him and reached for my report card. The other students teased me and told me I was dumb. A kid named Darell locked my arms behind my back and ribbed me about my Fs. He called me stupid. When I got loose, I snatched my report card. It was torn in pieces. Later I sat with Darell during lunch. He pointed at me.

"That boy got all Fs."

The table laughed. I reached over and fisted Darell in the face. I'd beat him until his lips were bleeding. Once again I got put out of school.

I kept praying to God, asking him for guidance, but it seemed like he never answered my prayers. So I decided to forget about trying to change. I was a failure. I was never going to make it.

"Moon, what happened?" my grandmother asked again as she held my hand in her room in Houston.

I turned my head away and pushed back all the memories of failure.

"Nothing Grandma, this just the new me. I can't read and I'll never learn. I'm not thinking about change right now."

My grandmother turned my face towards hers and looked me in the eyes, "I love you grandson and I'm praying that you change your life. I believe that you are going to change because it's been in your heart to do it. You just need time."

"I don't want to grandma. This is just who I am."

My grandmother prayed for me. I did want to change, but I didn't know how.

After we finished praying, Raheem arrived. I tried to talk with him, but he was angry. He cussed me out and told me to stay out of his face. I was hurt. I asked him what the problem was, but he punched me on my arms and legs. I backed off. I never saw Raheem angry and didn't think he would turn on me. But I'd been wrong about Raheem. He did have worries. He didn't have it all *in place*. He wouldn't talk to me for days.

I stopped hanging with my cousin and went my own way because I figured I could run a better game than he could. At school, I still went with a lot of girls and walked the halls like the prince of ghetto fabulous. But then Naomi stopped calling when she found out that I was playing mind games. Some of her friends stopped talking to me.

Mostly I smoked weed with Nick. I smoked until I couldn't feel myself. I was trying to get away from the world. The problem was that the escape never lasted. There's no way to run from this world. The only thing we can do is face it and overcome our biggest challenges, whether they're family problems or accepting ourselves.

Finally, my grandmother told me why Raheem was mad: His momma hadn't sent him a check. At the time I didn't understand why he didn't just tell me. At 17, I do. I think Raheem was embarrassed about asking his mother for money in front me; he wanted to make me think life was easy and that he could control the women around him. He wasn't a man, but a kid who was looking for a life. Raheem didn't understand that living is about helping others. It's not only about satisfying our own needs but about knowing that we've made someone else's life better.

I would like to be able to say that I learned something that day, something about manhood and responsibility. I'd like to be able to describe how a light went off in my head and I knew I had to make a real change in my life or I'd end up like Raheem—waiting for the next check. But that kind of epiphany was still two years off. At the time I thought that if change happened, it would be from talking to my grandmother and from going to church. However, real change comes from within. It would not be until I saw a vision for my future, one made from the heart and not borrowed from a music video, that I could start to grow. Even then I had to give up the negative forces I knew would keep me from reaching my goal: Friends, drugs, anger.

I'm not the only one who's grown. Now if I ask my grandmother where Raheem's at, she says he's staying with his baby momma or at his job. The mistakes and experiences he's faced have taught him what it takes to be a real man: Work, responsibility and respect. You have to know the first two before you earn the third.

Promised Endeavors

by Darielle Trotter

Standing in the freezer aisle of the grocery store, I made a promise to my mother. I told her I would go to college. I was only six years old, and so I did not really understand the significance of my words. While walking through the aisles, she told me that education was the way out. A college degree could change our lives. At the time, I didn't think it would be such a hard promise to keep. I also didn't understand how far away college was from kindergarten. I thought going to college would be just another activity like the coloring we did in class before taking a nap.

For many years, I grew up in an unstable household filled with abuse and drugs. School became my escape, a safe haven. It was the one place where I was not only stress-free but accomplished. I felt in control at school. I made everyone proud with my grades and my teachers praised me, giving me the calm, motherly attention that wasn't always available at home. Every time I did right, I was rewarded, from reading all the books in the library to receiving the highest recognition for my GPA, "Ms. Mason Elementary."

My mother also did her part to help me keep my promise. She always stressed the importance of education. I was never allowed to miss school, even if I was sick. I could not make grades lower than Bs. Cs meant being grounded and confined to my room for a week after school during which time I was to write *I will get better grades* five hundred times. My mother always made it clear that it was hard being a young parent without an education. She had to work two jobs, both low-paying, just to make ends meet. She had almost no time to relax or devote to herself. She was caught in an exhausting cycle that I witnessed each day.

My stepfather's abuse, both mental and physical, erupted constantly. Almost every night he and my mother would fight. My stepfather also used drugs, which made him lash out at everyone. Witnessing and being subject to the madness at home motivated me to excel at school. I told myself that when I grew up, I would go to college and my life would be different.

Eventually, I came to understand that my mother's lack of an education made her feel trapped and dependent on my stepfather. Because my stepfather's job paid more, he felt he had the right to control our household as he saw fit. My mother, worn down and without confidence in her ability to stand on her own, gave in. She always said if she had more money, we would leave him. She regretted not having pushed herself to go further in school. If she had a college degree, she told me, she could get a better job. She would have seen herself as someone with options. But without the confidence that comes from higher education, it was easy for him to tear her down and drag her through the mud.

Realizing my worth and my mother's worth was a lesson we had to learn the hardest way possible. We both now know that we cannot depend on someone else to make our lives worth living. I'm going to find a job that I love and that pays enough so that I can live comfortably. I plan to be confident and independent. No one will be able to use me or my mother in those ways again. Going to college is a crucial first step in learning about myself, my potential and what I can do to help take care of my family.

It's been 12 years since I promised my mother I would go to college. I'm a senior now with applications out at 14 colleges. I'm not the oldest, but I'm determined to be the example for my four brothers. No one in my family has a college degree, so it's up to me to be the voice of encouragement and experience for the next generation. I plan to be the one who sets the expectation and tells my children, grandchildren, nieces, and nephews that they will be attending college. Instead of being cashiers and janitors, my family will take on the new roles as business owners, doctors, and other successful professionals. Through education, we can redefine ourselves as individuals who are not seen as replaceable, low-skilled workers but as valued assets with unique and talented minds.

Empowering Our Youth

by Herbert Perryman

> "Education either functions as an instrument which is used to facilitate integration of the younger generation into the logic of the present system and bring about conformity or it becomes the practice of freedom."
>
> —Dr. Paulo Freire, *Pedagogy of the Oppressed*

Brazilian civil rights activist and thinker, Dr. Paulo Freire, wrote these words in the 1960's to describe the abilities of education to produce either conventional, tame citizens or conversely, innovative and even rebellious thinkers. Freire's text has sold over 750,000 copies worldwide and is still used as one of the foundations for critical pedagogy. His words make me wonder about the aims and effects of New Orleans public education and why it is that despite talk and reforms designed to spark change, our system continues to fail to inspire its citizens towards freedom. This freedom allows students to make their own choices; when educated, we tend to make choices that are more beneficial for us.

The school system today creates struggle, rather than the freedom that Freire advocates, because it doesn't encourage children to want to learn. As youth, peer pressure is very overwhelming and if there's no one motivating you to do better, it's very rare that you'll motivate yourself.

In its ranking of high school performance in math and science, *The Huffington Post* reports Louisiana is far below the national average. Our state is third to last when it comes to supplying our students with a competitive education in these critical fields. Only Mississippi and West Virginia score lower. On a recent *US News and World Report's* ranking of the top 100 public high schools in America, New Orleans appears only once. Benjamin Franklin, a math- and science-centered magnet school, ranks number 27. Texas, New York and California each contain more than 10 of the top 100 schools. Since New Orleans has been able to get a school listed in the top thirty, it shows that we can produce quality learning environments.

Unfortunately, we do not consistently hold ourselves to this standard. I know that there are more than 600 students in New Orleans who could create another school worthy of being ranked in America's top 100. So why don't we take education seriously? Are we just not willing to do so?

As a nation, particularly as New Orleanians, we should strive to set goals not merely standards. Setting standards instead of setting goals is the biggest problem with the New Orleans school system. We tend to put a limit on what we can achieve and not progress past those limits. Standards are an approval model, whereas goals demand specific results and achievements. The difference between the two is that when doing something to the best of your ability, you should always strive to surpass standards and to reach goals.

Standards create room for slack. This kind of system keeps us trapped as learners because we limit ourselves. This trap is particularly difficult to escape from in underprivileged places like New Orleans. New Orleans is known as an impoverished city and was recently considered the murder capital of the USA. As a majority, we rely on the government to support us in all of our needs. Many of our students end up in jails or prisons. A teen living a hard life can only be saved by a knowledgeable mentor. There are students who could have been saved with just a small amount of encouragement; instead, they ended up going through our jail system. We have to take responsibility for the whole of society, starting with the impoverished. Under-resourced students need a foundation and specific goals. Instead, we've unequally distributed the effort and resources needed to create the same quality of education for all students.

After Hurricane Katrina, New Orleans received hundreds of millions of dollars to bring our city up to par. Unfortunately, giving our schools influential titles doesn't change the way the school performs or even how efficient the school is. Terms like *college prep, charter* and *magnet* should put us in the mindset of working to achieve excellence; however, all too often these labels aren't backed up with results. In the nearly seven years since Katrina, I've attended a half dozen schools, each time following what promised to be a better institution. Only two have delivered: Samuel J. Green Charter School and the International High School of New Orleans. Both did what great schools do: They changed my life.

The first school I attended directly after Katrina seemed promising: It offered a nicely renovated building and loving teachers. However, the school was in a tough section of town and soon there were substantial behavioral problems. The hopes for a new and revitalized start were overpowered by negative attitudes. Teachers soon let the students have their way because there was literally no way to stop the students. Students showed absolutely no respect for adults in the school. They would stand on desks in the classroom. There were several gang fights. The children were just ruthless. No, students can't overpower the teachers by themselves, but with the help of higher authority they could effectively run the school. The disciplinarians in the school weren't doing their part when it came to controlling and punishing students. When students acted out, there were no consequences. Instead of getting suspended, they basically had a "free pass." This system soon backfired. Teachers felt as if they had no authority over the students and came to resent the administration.

I then spent two years at an academy. This new school promised not only an education, but also brotherhood. According to their motto, scholarship, innovation, vision, results, and heart were the school's values. In truth, the academy's vision went haywire. The students and teachers were in agreement on one point only: No one would be required to meet the stated goals. Still we all passed, continuing on in a system that did nothing to prepare us for college or the professional world. The school was located in trailers and fenced in on all sides. Because they felt like prisoners, many students acted as criminals. Although they came into the school year ready to learn, they finally gave into the uncaring attitude the administration displayed. Enslaved by their own ignorance, they yelled at teachers, refused to do their work and set fire to classrooms. So much for brotherhood.

My search for a school that offered a quality education finally led me a place that takes learning seriously: International High School. I remember the first day of school was just as instructional as the rest of the year. International makes it clear that we are to be productive from the time we step through the school doors until we hear the final bell. Like most New Orleans schools, International sums up its standards in a motto: Respect, rigor, and responsibility. However, at International these words are more than a motto to please the ears, they are a living philosophy.

The diversity of the school was a totally new experience for me, a young African-American male, who had until that time, attended predominantly black schools. This diversity has played a major role in attaining a quality education. Hearing people speak many languages sets a different environment for the whole school. The students who were bilingual weren't necessarily black or white but of different and sometimes mixed ethnicities. About half the students are exchange students.

The exchange students blended in with the American students because they had learned the key to relating with people from other places. They knew our language and social customs; they were well-mannered and showed a willingness to respect others' beliefs. They set an environment of productive learning and often took education more seriously than many of the New Orleans students I had encountered before.

In communicating with the exchange students that came to my school, I began to think that I was capable of visiting another country and display the same level of adaptation. In

May of 2010, I was fortunate enough to be selected for an educational research trip to Montreal, Canada, sponsored by Urban League College Track. Like International High School, the Canadian conference our team visited stood on the same core principals: That the entire population deserves a quality education. The conference was held at McGill University, the seventeenth-highest ranked college in the world.

Canada's multiculturalism was a revelation to me. I was able to see people from different backgrounds and cultures interact. In Canada, everyone was bilingual; all students learn English and French and then a third language as well. Its work laws further reinforce this language requirement: All employees must be proficient in English and French. Canadians put education first and deliver it to their students at a competitive level. Seeing the Canadians speak two languages fluently and receive a superior education showed me how free they were. A quality education comes at no cost for Canadians. Freedom is given to everyone equally and as a result, they make better decisions as a society. As a New Orleanian, I was stunned to learn that many Canadians don't even lock their doors when they go into their homes because they view such fear as a form of enslavement. They would rather leave their doors unlocked and trust their fellow citizens.

Setting up our youth to receive second language learning for the first time in high school is just too late. There is power and freedom in language learning. It goes outside of the classroom, and it opens the world. We need to put secondary language learning on the front line. As children, we hold the future possibilities for our city, and for a long time now, New Orleans has had much work to do. We have been too stuck in our ways. Freedom for all must be the reality for students here. Language learning, multiculturalism and setting goals are all essential in providing students with a stronger education system in New Orleans. It's not enough to say we put education first. We must actually commit to empowering our youth.

The Monkey and The Moon

by Carl Allridge

It was a black night on the island. The reflection of the moon shone on the surface of the ocean and the animals in the jungle were curious of both the ball in the sky and the one floating on the water.

"Why is the moon down here if it is also in the sky?" the ground animals asked.

"Why is the moon in the sky if it is also down there?" the tree animals asked.

So all the animals decided they should ask the wisest mind on the island, the one known as "The Philosopher of the Universe." The Philosopher happened to be a monkey who obtained his knowledge by observing the island from the tallest tree.

The animals asked him, "Why is the moon in the sky if it is also in the water?"

The monkey looked into the clouds as if they would uncover the answer and the clueless animals all began to worry that the philosopher wouldn't know the reason. They waited. Eventually the the monkey looked down at the animals.

"I have no knowledge of this phenomenon," he said, "but that doesn't mean I can't solve the problem."

The monkey went to get a better look at the second moon. He stood on a tall cliff that seemed to allow him to grab the moon with his bare hands. The monkey was thinking that if he could take the moon, he would be able to observe it. So he reached out and tried to grab it. But he also knew that if he stretched too far, gravity would pull him and he'd fall.

Instead, he looked down the cliff to where the other mystery moon lay. He was hypnotized for never had he been this close to the moon. Recklessly, he tried to grab it. Suddenly, he fell into the water. The orb waited just ahead of him on the water's surface. He tried to swim after it, but eventually drowned. Foolishly, he thought he could catch the moon.

The Burden of Life

by Nicoi Pierce

The pain of life is its death, and the circumstances that lead to that death, with words and actions true and spoken for the dead. The burden of life can be too much to carry. Splinters and thorns penetrate the skin of our shoulders. It is a heavy load, marking us with scars forever to be exposed and only partially ignored. This burden can lead us to thoughts of loss and worthlessness.

That thought of being fed up with everything. That thought of your mother's last breath before being escorted into the heavens above. Her soft whisper, the gentle, frail touch of her hand clasping yours. Her worried voice when she told you she got laid off from her job as she stared at the shoes you begged daddy for, paid with money from the job he no longer possessed. The tears that ran halfway down your cheek before you wiped them away. The secrecy and pained voices, the silent mental prayers and the twenty dollar bill passed from a fiend to a hand, one that has never experienced loss, to a hand that is a living work of profanity and ignorance. Minds dwelling in war. Minds dwelling in unpretentious love.

The thought of that final word spoken, and other words: Letters, phrases spilling from your tongue and filling the room with hatred and unattained motivation. The knife held in unclean hands, its blade gliding across a thigh that couldn't be cleaned, but covered with a second skin of her mother's, father's and brother's blood. And now her own. The gesture is quick, a slice at the throat, like cutting through a ripe pomegranate. Bright red oozing from all sides, spilling onto black roses tightly grasped in the little brother's hands. His heart was too broken to bear tears for the burial of the only one he had left.

The burden of life cannot be defined by intelligence, but by suffering. By a black man, incarcerated, solitary confinement, for the possession of drugs. A razor slipped under his door by the supposedly superior white hand, whispering to the inmate that his people weren't killing themselves fast enough. Or the girl, molested by someone she put her trust in, now battling the undeniable persuasiveness of suicide. Or the girl, who has never once suffered her own loss, but suffered for those who have lost, the girl who has it made, but in actuality, wants nothing at all.

The burden of life is a struggle. Most people would say especially for those of color. I disagree, because now people sans color battle the same frustrations as any other race. Yes, black people are undermined and tormented, but a white boy can't walk through what's called "The hood" today or though a school hall filled with chocolate faces without feeling the threat that will later drive him into a coma. He will be buried deep, topped with an engraved tombstone pronouncing his innocence.

The ignorance of people who believe a single individual has it easy intrigues me.

Snatch and Run

by Troy Simon

I'm glaring out of the windows during math class, thinking about the last eight days of my life. I'd spent them in prison. It was a place I'd been before, but only for tapping in the Quarter, never for theft. I knew the consequences for stealing, but I chose to ignore them. I should have never jacked that woman's purse. I should have just walked off. How foolish I was, thinking that I could make a quick getaway through the crowds on Bourbon Street. But hindsight is perfect.

And now I'm stuck in seventh grade with this box-like computer around my right ankle. The police are able to track my every move.

My friends think the bracelet is silly. They crack jokes about how I took a bath with it on. How I sleep with it charging around my ankle. How I tuck and hid it with my school pants.

They rib me to cheer me up. However, everywhere I go, I'm embarrassed. Out on the streets I see how people watch me. They look at my face, but then their eyes drop down to check out my ankle.

The other students ask me questions: How did the cops arrest you? Did they slam you on the ground while you were handcuffed? Did they beat you? How did your friends get away? Did you snitch on them? How much money was in the purse? Did she know you were going to steal it?

Suddenly, our math teacher, Ms. Diane, yells across the room. "Leave that damn boy alone! Nosy children. Can't you see he's trying to talk?" She glares at the students. Ms. Diane's voice chases them back to their seats. She keeps her students in line. If any one talks out of place, she points the repercussions to them. No questions asked.

Ms. Diane sits back in her swivel chair and knits her eyebrows together. She crosses her legs under her beige skirt and slips her fingers through her long black hair. One of her black heels points from under her desk. Even though she wears blazers and skirts, she has told us who she is. *Don't get it twisted.*

I'm from the 7th Ward. "Go Troy!" she says, pointing a red nail at me. "Tell your story."

"Okay." I close my eyes and bring myself back to the sound of Lionel's voice. "It all starts like this."

* * * * * * *

My cousin Darnell blew the smoke from his weed cigarillo at my face. "We need money, son." Thin white trails flowed from his nose and mouth.

I stood with my right leg against Darnell's porch, thinking about how to come up with the money to pay Ruben. Ruben was 17, five years older than me, six years older than Darnell. We owed Ruben for taking the charge and lying to the cops and saying he'd stolen some hats from the Walgreens when it was us. The cops confiscated his taps and fifty dollars from his pockets and drove him to the juvie. Ruben called us before he got out and said he wanted triple for taking the charge. So now we had until sundown to come up with a hundred fifty dollars. Ruben was serious about getting his money. We had seen what happened to those who didn't pay up. Visible scars. Black eyes. Broken noses.

"Puff! Puff! Give!" James yelled and leaned in. Our friend snatched the cigarillo out of Darnell's hand.

"Y'all want to go tapping?" Darnell danced with his bare feet on the concrete porch.

"Yeah, son!" I said. I thought we could go down to the French Quarter and dance for money. We'd done it plenty of times before. Maybe this was our chance to pay Ruben back.

* * * * * * *

We left Darnell's house in the Bywater and went downtown to the Florida projects. We needed some nails to attach the taps to the bottom of our shoes. I heard that my girlfriend Niece was looking for me around the corner. I immediately decided to take a swing over there. I'd told Darnell and James I was coming back.

There's my girl, I said to myself as I walked inside the black gates and saw Niece sitting on the concrete steps of her aunt's porch. She was red skinned, short.

"Wuzzam!" I laughed.

Niece rolled her light brown eyes. "What! So that's how you talk to me now? Like I'm a stranger?"

We kissed and hugged. I ran down with her what I was about to do.

"Why Troy?" she demanded. She reminded me that I could get picked up by the cops. It had happened before.

"But I need the money," I explained. Over her shoulder, a dozen screaming kids ran after the ice cream truck.

"What about me?" she asked. "I need you." She leaned in closer to my side and softly rubbed her nose across my shoulder.

"I know."

The tension flooded out of me. Niece was my heart. She always kept me out of trouble when I couldn't think for myself. We hugged for a long time and kissed. But she held her ground. If I went along with them, she didn't want to be bothered with me anymore. She was tired of me listening to my friends and not her. She worried that something would happen to me; she had nightmares about me going to jail or getting jumped.

"We'll hang out next time," I told her. I could hear her breathing as I edged closer, tracing her nose with my lips. "I promise."

She pressed her head against my chest, then pushed herself off and moved down the porch. "See Troy, that's what I'm talking about! You always getting yourself into something that you don't have no business doing."

She was right. I needed to slow down, but there was no backing out of the situation with Ruben. Not this time. Darnell and James were depending on me, and it was getting late. "I'm sorry," I told her. "This my last time."

It was a lie. I knew tonight was just the beginning of how my life would end up. I was failing my classes. School wasn't the answer. I figured hustling the streets was the only future I had.

* * * * * * *

I met Darnell and James at the bus stop. James told me he'd borrowed some nails from Lionel, who would meet us in the Quarter. At that moment, I knew that there was going to be trouble. Lionel was 17 and known for jacking tourists out of their wallets. He would say, *They drunk any way. What they don't know won't hurt them.* But fighting the tourists when they were drunk wasn't cool, especially elderly men. One time when we were tap dancing together, the flow of money wasn't coming fast enough, so he called it quits, and snuck in the Hilton Hotel to steal Gameboys. In ten minutes he'd stolen two hundred and seventy dollars worth of stuff.

We'd hopped on the bus and saw the last person we wanted to see. Ruben sitting in the back. He pointed at the row in front of him, cocking his finger. Like obedient dogs, we all sat down.

"You got my money?" Ruben demanded, his jaw tightening into a hard edge. The light filtered through the window and lit his eyes. Acne scarred his forehead. Beneath his dry lips, a chain of pus-covered bumps erupted across his chin.

"No, not yet." I said. A chill slithered down my back.

"If you don't have my money by tonight, my boys and I will beat James, Darnell and you to death." He leaned in. "And that's a promise."

I kept silent. James and Darnell bit their tongues.

"I'll be on Bourbon watching y'all." Ruben said, pushing his index finger in my face.

In my head I saw the bloody face of a guy who was late paying Ruben for weed. Ruben had the guy beat half to death, left him with a broken nose, a busted lip and a swollen jaw. We had to pay on time or turn out like the other guy. None of us said anything, but we were afraid. I knew we wouldn't make one hundred fifty dollars by just dancing. That was wishful thinking. So I thought about Lionel's way, about snatching a purse. It was worth the try. Even if I was caught, jail would keep me safe from Ruben's fists.

* * * * * * *

In the Quarter, we saw Lionel was already dancing. He wore a white shirt, black jeans and yellow Adidas that showed off his footwork.

"What took ya'll so long?" Lionel asleep.

"The bus!" Darnell replied.

Lionel paused and caught his breath. Sweat covered his face and soaked his shirt. His arms bulged from weightlifting. Across his neck was a tattoo that read, *Money Over Everything*. His jeans sagged from the weight of the change in his pocket.

Lionel and I danced together while James and Darnell tapped alone. But no matter how hard we'd tried, the money wasn't flowing fast enough. After two hours, we had only fifty dollars and change.

Darnell threw his money box on the ground. "This ain't working. We got to fight Ruben."

"Yeah, man. Ruben got me bent," James added, pointing a finger at my direction.

I sat on the curb and stared across the street at the trash blowing along the sidewalk. I knew we could fight Ruben together, but I also knew that he wouldn't be scared off. He would just wait until we were alone and then come back twice as hard. He'd probably knock my teeth out and fracture my nose. Maybe he would break my jaw and crack open my chin. Maybe he'd just kill me. I refused to take that chance. Pressing my fingers against my temple, I knew we were out of options. We had to steal.

"I got a plan," I said.

I told Lionel about Ruben's threat. He agreed stealing was our only chance now. In truth he seemed as if he was looking forward to teaching me.

"You ready to learn something?" Lionel asked, his eyes blazing with excitement. His cheekbones tightened with the force of his smile.

I glanced nervously. "Yeah, I'm ready."

We walked Bourbon Street looking for a corner bar, a place with two exits, so I wouldn't have to stop and double back. I told them I would steal the purse. I believed it was my fault that we couldn't pay Ruben on time. Either I'd steal a purse and we could pay Ruben, or I'd get caught and go to jail. Either way, I'd earn respect and save myself from being Ruben's punching bag. I knew it was a mistake to volunteer. I'd never snatched a purse before. Who knew what tourists might have hidden under their clothes? A can of pepper spray. A knife. A gun.

"All you got to do is snatch and run," Lionel told me. "Whatever you do, don't look back. It slows you down."

He gave me some tips: Keep my momentum. Grab the purse with one hand and pull it hard, then tuck it beneath my arms. Keep my face pointed forward so she wouldn't get a good look. I was to wait for his signal, three waves over his ear, then move. We had already picked our purse.

Snatch and run. Snatch and run. Then the adrenaline took over and pumped through my veins. I could hear my pulse beating in my ears, drowning out the sounds of Lionel's voice. I was blocking everything else out, focussing in on the task.

Suddenly, I ran without Lionel's signal. I grabbed and yanked the woman's purse from the bar counter. Someone pulled at my shirt. I felt the hem rip. Glass shattered on the floor. The woman fell off her stool. But I kept running. Behind me, I heard her scream. A man yelled, *Stop him!* as I jumped into the crowd on Bourbon. I ran full speed and never looked back.

When I reached the edge of the Quarter, I let myself pause to catch my breath. I looked at black bag in my right hand, just to make sure it was still there. James, Darnell and Lionel saw me run and found me.

"How much?" James asked, pointing at the bag.

"Open it man!" Darnell said.

"Y'all better split to, boy!" Lionel told us.

I should have listened to Lionel. Instead we stood where we were. There was a long pause as I opened the purse. I fished around in the bag and came up with a credit card and a license. An identification card. There was no cash.

Darnell punched a set of wooden doors. "Man!"

Lionel laughed while James and I sat in disbelief.

"Now what?" James asked.

Snatching the purse was our last chance to pay Ruben. We were in serious trouble. Niece was right. I needed to slow down and think out my options. Now it was too late. We couldn't stick around the Quarter. Our only hope was gone.

We all went home in silence. I was angry that we let ourselves get bullied by Ruben. I was even angrier that I'd let my fear convince me to steal. It was time to stand up for ourselves. We couldn't spend our lives wrestling against fate. Even if we choose to run from our problems or ignore them, they'd only build and destroy us. I realized that all I'd ever done was run. I was so afraid of getting hurt by someone else that I ended up hurting myself. Now it was my time to fight.

When we made it to the projects, Lionel went home. The beef with Ruben wasn't his. I told Darnell and James I wasn't hiding anymore. They agreed to sit on Ruben's porch and wait with me. Beside the house, the garbage can had been overturned and wrappers blew across the side street. We sat watching, but Ruben never showed up. The sky had grown black; it was time to go home. We stood up from the porch, feeling as though we had escaped. Suddenly he turned the corner.

Ruben cracked his neck and pointed his finger like always. "Where's my money, son?"

I looked down. "We don't have it."

All the tough talk about standing up evaporated. Before Ruben could speak again, we did what we always did. Ran.

"Come here!" Rueben yelled behind us.

We split. James ran in an abandoned building, Darnell to his house. When I looked back, I could see Ruben gaining on me. My baggy jeans fell from my waist and my large shirt covered my elbows. My street gear was slowing me down. My heart burned. Suddenly, I tripped and stumbled into a fence.

Ruben grabbed me by my shirt. "Get up!"

My courage was gone. "Please don't hurt me," I begged, stumbling over my words.

His fingers snapped at my collar, ripping it off its seam. His breath smelled like an ashtray. "Shut up. You take me for a joke?"

I shook my head. Ruben dug through my pockets, looking for change. He slipped my crumbled cigarillo into his pocket. He held up my tap nails, then threw them in the grass.

"Where's the money?" he demanded.

"I don't have it." I kept my head down. I was too afraid to even look at him.

The police car pulled up so quietly that even Ruben didn't see it until it was close. Ruben released his fingers from my shirt. He cracked his neck and whispered, "Pretend we're brothers."

Two cops stepped out of the vehicle. "Get on the ground!"

I didn't say anything, turning to Ruben for a sign. Sweat trailed down his neck. A smile pulled his skin, revealing his broken teeth. I stared at him, hoping to get his attention. He held his hands up as if the cops' words confused him, but kept a straight face. One of the cops pulled out his black stick from his belt. The other cop's hand hovered over the gun at his waist. These were no fat, donut-eating cops. They looked like bodybuilders. These cops were cut and taller than Ruben.

"He's just my li'l brother," Ruben told them. "We were just playing. That's all."

Ruben smiled and put his arm over my shoulder. I pretended to follow along, leaning into him. All of a sudden one of the cops rushed us. He grabbed Ruben and pushed his arms behind his back.

"That's my brother, man!" Ruben wrestled.

"You're wanted for arrest!" The cop said.

The other officer dragged me by my pocket, murmuring beneath his breath. He twisted my arm and threw me in the back seat. My head slammed against the window. The cop shut the door. I saw them talking through the glass. The cop who shoved Ruben was holding him down on the hood of the car. The other yelled in his face. A crowd watched on the corner, others from their porches. When I sat up, I looked at my shirt. The fabric was torn in several places.

Suddenly, a cop opened the door. "Sit back," he told me. "We're going to the station."

The cell was freezing. The iron bunk covered most of the space in the room. The toilet was covered in urine, its inside clotted with feces. Gang signs scarred the walls. Some read, *Blood Game, Young Mafia* and *Uptown*. I drew my fingers along the walls, trailing the dents. Then I sat on a small wooden bench. The ceiling was dotted with wads of tissue paper. I couldn't sleep. I was put on trial for two days before the jury convicted me. The judge sentenced me to three months for purse snatching. He told me I would have to serve my community by cleaning the streets. While on probation, I'd have to wear an ankle bracelet.

*   *   *   *   *   *   *

When I finish the story, my friend Terrance sits back in his chair. "Man, I am just happy you didn't get hurt."

"I know, right?" I say.

"You could have been hurt bad," another student says.

Suddenly, Ms. Diane starts to teach the class. She reads from a paper in her hand and presses the dry erase marker against the white board.

"All right class, turn to page 162 in your math books," she says. "We're solving exponents."

I lean back, twist my dreads, and cross my leg. I feel the weight of the ankle bracelet. I stare out of the window as my teacher's voice fades. I hear Lionel again, his words echoing across my conscience. *Snatch and Run. Snatch and Run.* I knew if I continued to steal, I would end up in jail. I knew if I continued to be influenced by my friends, I'd end up in worse situations. The only choice was to make a new decision, my own decision, one that wasn't about either stealing or running.

That life leads to drugs or jail or the cemetery. I thought about the road I was taking. I knew I had to find a different path, perhaps even forge my own way.

* * * * * * *

Six years have passed since I was arrested and decided I had to make a change. Not everyone came to the same realization as I did. The young men I knew have become sad and familiar statistics. "Darnell" and "James" have dropped out of high school. "Lionel" was gunned down while mugging someone in the Ninth Ward. "Ruben" became a thief and an addict and recently, was shot to death by a drug gang.

As for me, I am changed, have let myself be changed, by education. I have put in the long hours required to begin to make up for all the years that I couldn't read or write, all the the years I believed I couldn't learn. I have attended afterschool and weekend programs for college-bound youth and surrounded myself with mentors. I have also turned to writing as a way of understanding my troubled past. Last December, I was awarded a four-year scholarship to Bard College through the Posse Foundation. No more Snatch and Run. When I graduate, I plan to be an elementary teacher so that I can mentor and direct young people in the right direction.

Part II

Poetry

Initial Thought

by Tia Harris

When you look at me
All you see is a pretty face,
Thick hair and a nice smile,
But really, I'm so much more.

I'm smart. I'm nerdy.
I'm loud but shy.
I'm my own person;
I don't let anything control me.

When you see the world,
All you see is danger,
The murders and the violence,
But there's so much more to it than that.

It's vast. It's rigorous.

It's adventurous. It's discovering,

Always searching

For the answers that avoid us.

When the world looks at you,

All it sees is the welfare,

The Medicaid and the unemployment,

But I know you are so much more.

You are unique. You are intelligent.

You are energetic.

You are strong-willed.

You are the gem of your parents.

You are my fellow human being.

Without the inside,

Our initial thought is only the outside.

But if we look deeper,

we see the complexity underneath.

When I Grow Up

by George Aidoo

When I grow up I want to be a Ringmaster,

But I'm allergic to dirty animals.

When I grow up I want to be a Rocket Surgeon,

But that's not a real profession.

When I grow up I want to be a Computer Technician,

But how do you spell disaster?

When I grow up I want to be a Poet,

But what rhymes with orange?

When I grow up I want to be a Writer,

But then I'd have to actually write.

When I grow up I want to be a Teacher,

But I hate kids.

When I grow up I want to be a Mathematician,

But math has too many problems.

When I grow up I want to be a Counselor,

But PEOPLE HAVE TOO MANY PROBLEMS.

When I grow up I want to be a...

Ask me later.

Tangents

by George Aidoo

Tangent #1:

If the world was really made for us just to leave it, why care what people say or do?

Tangent #2:

The fact is you can't do anything you put your mind to.
Example: Hugging a bear.

Tangent #3:

You're not what you eat. You're what you hate.

Tangent #4:

If you die, someone will replace you.

Tangent #5:

Nothing's personal if you tell someone.

Tangent #6:

What is true if everything is false?

Tangent #7:

Mom: Money isn't worth anything, son.

Me: But everything isn't free.

Tangent #8:

The saying "You're dead to me" doesn't work if the person is still alive.

Tangent #9:

I thought about it for a second, but it's not worth thinking about.

Tangent #10:

Girls decide to break up with me on my birthday.

Tangent #11:

The dream is not as good as you think.

Tangent #12:

If I had superpowers, I would have superpowers.

Tangent #13:

Random irrelevance.

Tangent #14:

I hated writing before I started having an imagination.

Truth or Hope?

by Lanesa Barabino

Truth…

May be brutal

May be helpful

But after truth,

What else?

You're left with a wound,

It may heal, clean or scar.

Truth is a sometimer,

It may be an uncertainty.

LIES…

The truth

can be made up to

please the ears and

help the heart.

The truth…

Truth can kill.

But what else!

When you're hurt

And depressed from truth's wrath,

What do you do?

I'll tell you.

Use hope.

Like the hope of a kid

In Santa and the Tooth Fairy.

Hope keeps you together

Through some of the most

brutal times.

So what do you want?

The truth of a lie or belief

or your hope in knowing

and understanding your beliefs?

The hope of the nation

is nothing

without the truth of reality.

So I choose

Both.

Cliché

by Lanesa Barabino

Who am I?

Such a cliché question,

but seriously who or what makes me, me?

A passion for dance?

Cliché

Curly hair?

Cliché.

Love to shop?

Hate to stop?

Love my body?

Love my speech?

Cliché.

Cliché.

Cliché.

What sets me apart from every other girl that may...

walk by me,

talk of me,

care for me,

lie on me,

tease me,

help me.

Ha, never.

It took a while to analyze,

to pull my life together and criticize.

I'm not a cliché.

No one cries like me

nor stutters so beautifully.

No one dances like me

every shake a meaning

or laughs like me

such continuous squeal

or draws like me

every stroke an emotion.

Do you see what I see?

I'm not like anyone else

I'm only unmistakably,

undeniably

me.

Letter to My Unborn Baby

by Briana Brown

Dear Elliot. Benjamin. Sebastian. Robyn. Or Bella,

Before I could hold you

Before I could comfort you when you cried

Before I could hear you speak your first words…

Before you could crawl

Before you could stand

Before you could walk

Your knees, feet, and legs were taken from you.

Before I could see you off on your first day of school

Before I could sit down and help you with your homework

Before I could applaud and watch you

Perform in the school play…

You were gone.

Before you could fall in love for the first time

And cry after the break up

Before I could wipe your tears and tell you everything would be ok

Before I could hear you speak of your hopes and dreams

Before I could marvel at any awards you may have received

Or see you walk across the stage and smile with your college degree...
You were gone before you were here.
I wish I could have tucked you in at night
And I wish that in the morning, for breakfast I could have given you the World on a silver platter.

But I couldn't feed you because
I didn't have the money
And I couldn't tuck you in because
I was asleep myself
And I couldn't wipe your tears because
I was too busy crying
And I couldn't help you with homework because
I had some of my own.
I wish I could have given you the best
Life possible. But I couldn't...
I wish I would have met you, but not
At age 16.

Lost

by Andrew Gould

I feel as if I'm coming closer to the end

But my mind gets lost with the wind

I feel something so real, but I tend to not comprehend

Because I don't know where my mind went.

It goes to this place where I am asleep.

It feels as if I am laying in a cave, six feet deep.

I'm lost on a road without any transportation

I don't know where to travel

because there's a question on my navigation.

I try to read but the writing is horrific

It's looking like hieroglyphics

Now I'm lost, I don't know what to think

I mostly stay afloat, but what happens if I sink?

When I'm in this position I go into that 'what if' state

And start thinking. What if there is faith?

Is there a reaper that decides

Whether you live or die?

Whenever my mind goes into this position

Everything I strive for loses all attention

I start talking so I don't have to think

Then this negative thinking starts to shrink

Then I say why think this is all irrelevant

I try to explain it to everybody

but my mind doesn't leave any evidence.

Therefore, leaving me lost.

Imperfectly Great Leader

by Robert Burnside, Jr.

I am a Leader

An African

American Leader

Might be young

But I understand

Not to find fault

Find a remedy

Deep down

A good person

True identity

Though I might give up on something seemingly good

It means that I make room for something great

Some people say they're real

But they pretend and imitate

I am not a political leader with legislative authority

But a young leader with aspirations

To demonstrate credibility, show integrity,

Take responsibility

I am not here for perfection

But for direction

Your Heart Will Be Hard To Grasp

by Janai McGill

Your heart will be hard to grasp.

Whenever it seems close,

It slips a little further away.

You tease me and let me think

I own your heart,

But whenever I try to hold on,

You say, *It's too soon*.

Your heart will be hard to control.

It never does what I ask it to.

It leaps and dodges constantly;

It cannot be trained.

Your heart will let me down.

I will think I have it disciplined.

I will think I am the master

But it will be me that is broken.

So before I let your heart hurt me again,

I'll simply have to let it roam.

Full of Flight

by Irene Beauvais

In memory of "Mooney" (1993-2010)

A public figure

tall with light brown skin

small, full lips

they stuck out like a kiss

a round big nose

a freshly cut fade

ready for the world

and full of flight

Swag in its definition

classic white tees and baggy jeans

some Jays for show

mostly the type

ready to show off

and full of flight

Want to see me?

You don't want to see me.

Chilling with his brother

never backed down from a challenge

Hit 'em with that #2 Popeye's chicken meal with extra fries!

gave 'em black eyes

That's when you knew

it was time to fly

Loved me, family, friends

protected his turf, his home

defended my honor when dude

didn't come correct.

Showed respect for oldies

made everyone laugh.

One thing was promised:

a time of flight

Nightmare

time shares money, moo-lah, *diñero*

making plans

dropping dimes.

The plan was to make something

Dream: _____

this life, a mission

a time of flight

Destruct of Creativity

by Irene Beauvais

Where did it go? I guess it left me

Loyalty, where it went cause all my loyals left me

Left me, that's where my loyals went

But they say that's when I should self destruct

Mind blown, that's my self destruct

Too completed to compete with these down grades

Help me! Help me! This is my self-destruct

Opened to things that could never be opened to

Died and died but lived to say let's party hard and die again

People say it's crazy, but what's crazy is that we're here again

People say it's crazy, but what's crazy is that we're here again

But what's crazy is that you try to remain a part of society,

when society is a part of you

If it's hard to comprehend let me explain

Society is made up of ordinary humans,

but why place yourself in something that's ordinary

Point stated!

People say the only time you understand

is when you know confusion firsthand

But at that point you will self-destruct

Blind but the force to see

what is only opened to what is said

Translate!

Blind but the force to see

what is only opened to what is said

So let your ears be your guide and listen

If everyone couldn't see

then only one's personality can be heard,

then would we be able to say we are society

But when you're different

do you stand a chance or will you self-destruct?

Countdown to self-destruction...5...4...3...2...1

As the count down stops and your loyals are gone

You're there to self-destruct and remain sane

Cause when you self-destruct, you become a part of society.

She Watches Me

by Irene Beauvais

I talked to her alone

When only my brain was awake

Tossing and turning

My cousin, she interrupted my dreams

Red skinned girl with long red hair

A perfect role model for me

She walked in the shadows

She said life is too short so live

Like she lived

Beyond orbital life

She traveled light years

Space, earth, heaven, and hell

She was with the living

Those who could really live

She orbed non-stop into different worlds

But her heart walked my world

Her voice whispered in my ear

Softly like the wind

Telling me to be strong and always hold on

She was my wind and air that gave me life

She lay there on the driver's side

Pressing the gas as shot rang out

It was too late for her leave

It was too early for her to go

She poured out her feeling to me

In my dreams

She said she saw it, lurking around the corner

She said she saw her self looking at her reflection

She knew that life for her was just beginning eternally

She said that she will visit me again

Telling me not to worry

Be brave and don't give in

And from that day I was never afraid to know

she watches over me

Hurricane

by Yasmien Brown

    Lights out

    in the dark,

    Dogs bark.

    Is this the end?

    My life has just begun.

    Outside, water rushes our way.

    I cry, yell, scream, pray.

    Lord, protect my family and I,

    Let us see another day.

    Help!

    Help!

    No one hears. My little voice a failure.

    Will someone save me before

    I drown,

Am murdered,

Die of hunger?

I can't take this

Babies crying,

People dying.

Someone rescue me.

Look for shelter or just lose hope?

Afraid of the dark,

Afraid for her family,

My mother gropes.

Should I Remain

by Yasmien Brown

Should you go first

and I remain

to walk the road alone,

I'll live in memories golden dear

with happy days we've known.

In spring I'll watch the roses red

in summer lilacs blue

in autumn when the brown leaves fall,

I'll catch a breath of you.

Should you go first

and I remain

on the path for battles to be fought,

each thing you've touched along the way

will always be a hallowed spot.

I'll hear your voice and see your smile

though blindly I may grope.

The memory of your loving heart

will busy me on with hope.

Should you go first

and I remain

to finish on my own the stroll,

no dark shadows shall creep in

to make this life less droll.

We've known so much happiness,

we've drunk our cup of joy.

Our memories are a gift of God

that death can never destroy.

Should you go first

and I remain

to walk the trail alone,

one thing we know for sure:

We meet again

in that bright land

beyond the golden shore.